Judy Thompson-Phillips

Charleston

Classic Coloring Book for Adults

Charleston
Classic Coloring Book for Adults

Page left blank for no pen bleed trough.

Page left blank for no pen bleed trough.

Page left blank for no pen bleed trough.

Page left blank for no pen bleed trough.

and Carolina Sayings... (with a drawl)

Welcome Y'all!

Loosely interpeted as y'all is 1 you all is 2 all y'all is 3 or more

Yes M'am
No Sir *mind your manners*

I do declare ...

Bless yore heart

Can be either sympathy or that's dumb.

honey
affectionate term

hey

Well, hush my mouth

amen!

graciuos!

goodness -

Coke
ALL carbonated beverages

whatchamacallit

hissy
fit
hysterical

Suppertime!

be back
before long, southern time

hug
yer
neck
come give me a hug

say the blessin'
always bless the food

goodnee!

I swannee!
polite swear word

Gimme some Sugar
affectionate kisses

ol' boy

over yonder *near or far*

Page left blank for no pen bleed trough.

Page left blank for no pen bleed trough.

Page left blank for no pen bleed trough.

Page left blank for no pen bleed trough.

Page left blank for no pen bleed trough.

Page left blank for no pen bleed trough.

Page left blank for no pen bleed trough.

and on the menu...

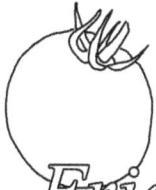

Shrimp n'Grits

Fried Green Tomaters

Collards

Biscuits

Gravy

Hoppin' John

FRIED OKRA

Sweet Tea

Mint Julip

Rice Puddin'

She-Crab Soup

Water-melon

Benne Seed Wafers

Oyster Roast

Cheese Straws

Pralines

Cracklin' Cornbread

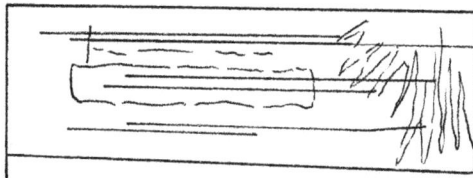

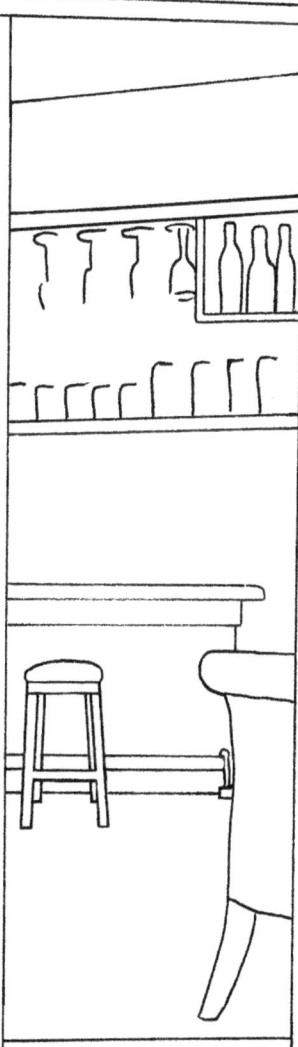

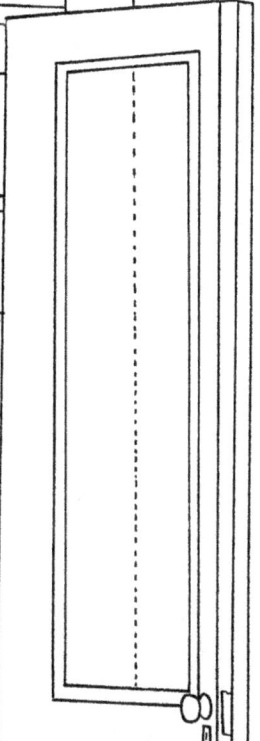

MENU
Shrimp
&
Grits

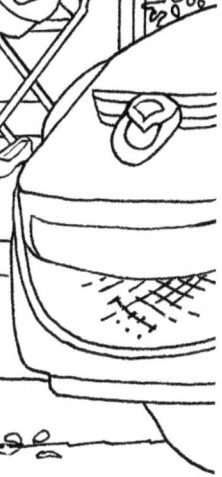

Page left blank for no pen bleed trough.

Page left blank for no pen bleed trough.

Page left blank for no pen bleed trough.

Page left blank for no pen bleed trough.

Page left blank for no pen bleed trough.

Page left blank for no pen bleed trough.

Page left blank for no pen bleed trough.

and places to see...

City Market

Gaillard Auditorium

Sullivans Island

Broad &Calhoun
East Bay
Meeting
&King
Streets

the Citadel

Fort Sumter

Isle of Palms

Spoleto

festival

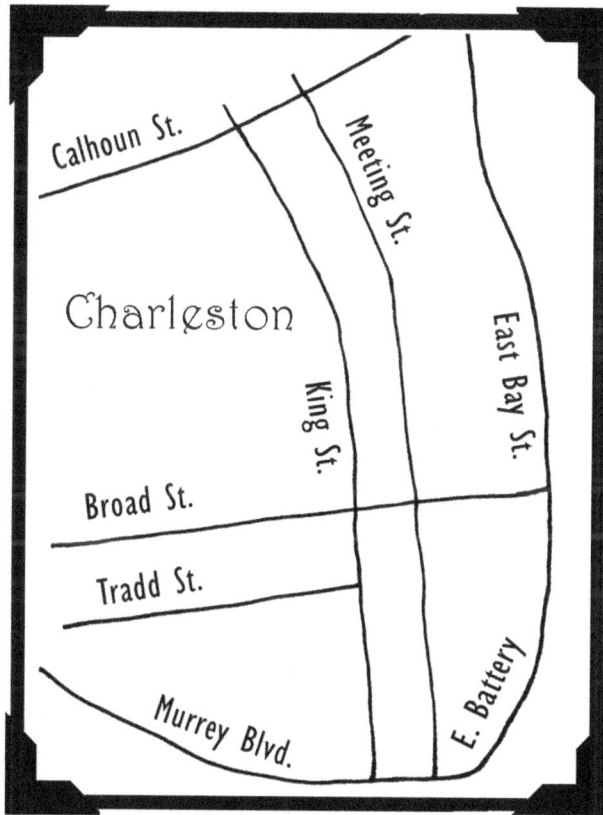

Calhoun St.

Meeting St.

Charleston

King St.

East Bay St.

Broad St.

Tradd St.

E. Battery

Murrey Blvd.

FOLLY BEACH

Patriots Point

Middleton Place

Charleston Museum

Page left blank for no pen bleed trough.

Page left blank for no pen bleed trough.

Page left blank for no pen bleed trough.

Page left blank for no pen bleed trough.

Page left blank for no pen bleed trough.

Page left blank for no pen bleed trough.

Color these pages "*YOUR WAY*" or look to hints below.

no. 32 Legare St. Sword Gates

Charleston's ironwork is famously beautiful and thankfully no longer needed to keep pirates out.

Walls are creamy white. Behind gates, shades of bluer-greens. Magnolia tree and flowers show a bit. It's leaves are quite dark with white flowers.

Beached Boats with clouds and birds

A beautiful day awaits. Skies are not always blue, feel free to experiment on a separate sheet and then allow your inner artist to "go for it"! Art is all about how you feel. Add more birds, or clouds perhaps? The sand is in beiges-grays.

Beached Boats

This scene allows you to make your own version of a perfect beach day. Sunset? Stormy?

Sky gets darker higher up, unless it's a storm, which may be darker at water horizon. A colorful rainbow or sunset is a good choice, as sunset is a peaceful time of day.

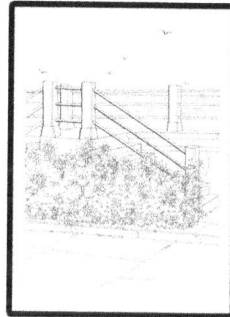

The Battery Wall Steps

This historic all important seawall looks out to Ft. Sumter.

Carolina blue sky reflects a bit deeper grayed color on the water. The wall walkway is a very pale gray-beige. The Cleome flowers are pretty pinks with smaller multi-colored plants at their base.

Biking on King St.

A cruise around the historic district by bicycle is so enjoyable, as you experience all the floral fragrance at your leisure.

Shades of the same color family may be good for the background. Add shadows in the foreground in shades of purple. Bright colors for the bikes.

Bougainvillea

A brilliantly colored tropical vine shows off ironwork, but be careful of the thorns.

Color away without too much regard for the lines as the crepe paper bracts are not true flowers, yellow stamens, leaves, deep green, the iron gray-blue to charcoal.

Charleston Veranda

The veranda is located to the side of homes to capture the cool breeze and shade, a respite from the heat and humidity.
Open spaces suggest calm, The back wall was a salmon color; the lilies, red and white and Lady Banks rose is creamy.

Dragonfly Bench

A bit of seclusion with style.

Shades of varying greens in the leaves with a touch of yellow in places. The bench, in shades of white-gray. Pottery colors and pillows as you like for your color scheme.

Color these pages *"YOUR WAY"* or look to hints below.

Gazebo and Carriage

White Point Gardens, on the Battery, is a historic and lovely, tranquil place.

Azaleas come in so many deep to pale colors of red. The far live oak trees of a pale grayed green, the gazebo is white with a tiled rich green roof.

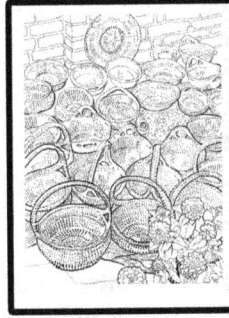

Market Baskets

Gullah basketmaking is a long tradition of local people. Finely made of pine needles and sweet grass.

The back part of the basket group was in shadow, so a bluer brown is used. Zinnia flowers are in yellows and reds.

Lyre Gate

Wonderful ironwork with a musical motif.

Buttery yellow walls, the courtyard colors are shaded darker. Ironwork, colored in various deep colors will make a more vibrant artwork. Roses, in your favorite color.

Medallion Gate

Most entryways have an elaborate and prestigious welcoming iron gate.

The ironwork, in many deep shades of nearly black, will add drama. Pastel whites for the home and various greens for leaves, as variety adds interest. Add flowers if you like more color.

Marsh Boat

For fishing or just to get away, a boat is a marvelous thing.

The original painting was at twilight, with subdued colors. Water, a pale olive green with a few hints of blue as the sky reflected. Marsh grass, shades of green with a few orange-brown tips. Boat, your choice.

Morris Island Lighthouse

Located at the end of Folly Island, the lighthouse is now used as a landmark.

The waving sea oats turn golden with their stalks in shades of browns and greens. The color of sky is reflected a deeper shade in the water. Lighthouse bands, from top, is off white, rusty brown and repeat.

Mysteria

She waits under arching wisteria and wonders at the wedding carriage. A tradition in Charleston, the newlyweds leave for their reception in a flower and ribbon festooned carriage.

This is the cover page, reference it for color choices.

Palmetto Sunset

Soft breezes and a "can't get better than this" view of a fabulous sunset! Life is good.

A light path from the setting sun is coming toward the chair on the left, the color is deeper on each side of it. The Atlantic color would be olive green to gray. Beach sand is gray-beige, palmetto trunks are brown-gray, palm fronds are greens and golds on the outer edges.

Color these pages *"YOUR WAY"* or look to hints below.

Porch Flags

Spring brings new buds to the trees as the flags wave their approval for a new year.

The S.C. flag is deep blue body with white designs. The limbs are brownish-green with a little reddish color near the buds. The porch ceilings are in a traditional pale blue to mimic the sky.

Rainbow Row - left

The perfect blend of ambience and southern hospitality, with pastel colors.

The nearer house is a medium dull rose, the next very pale green-gray, the next a buttery yellow. The Crepe Mrytle tree has blooms in one of the family of reds or white.

Rainbow Row -right

A favorite tourist attraction, all the rainbow colored houses are irresistably interesting.

The nearer house, pale yellow, the next is pale blue, then an olive green. Purple tones are useful in making shadows. The road has palmetto tree shadows and shadows under the cars.

Row House

Typical narrow street face but so many different house designs.

Red or pink Geraniums in the planters, pastel shades of whites-grays for the house. Deeper colors in the recessed areas. Play with making shadows from an unseen source.

Rhododendrons

These tough, yet so beautiful plants thrive in the sea air at the Battery.

From fushia to reds in the flowers. The underbrush is a jumble of browns. The wall is a rich creamy yellow with white-grayish ballistrades.

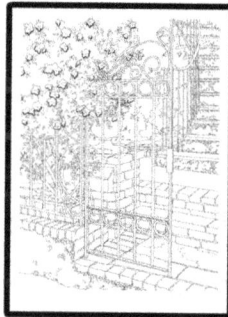

Cameilla Cascade

A fragrant welcome. A small ivy creeper dresses up the stair walls.

Various flower reds adorn this entry bush. Shades of color in the ironwork add interest. Close growing creeper on steps in greens.,brick, rose red.

Shrimp n' Grits

It's on the menu. This happy couple chose a shady spot to relax and enjoy the day.

The interior of the grill should a be dark muted color. The building, light pastel. The street gray and sidewalk beige with purple overlaid where there are shadows. The car color should compliment the scene. (ie. a bright red car maybe too strong and distracting)

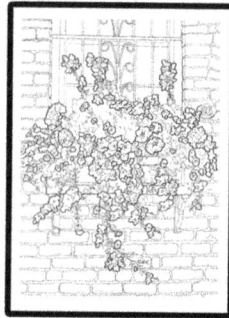

Window Box

Thanks to so many Charleston green thumbs and their delight-ful choices of assorted flowers.

Vary flower colors to suit. Colors of brick are muted reds but remember the mortar is a beige-gray. Add shadow under the box. The window inside is cool blue-gray, reflecting a bit of sky color.

Color these pages "*YOUR WAY*" or look to hints below.

Window Box -2

So many window boxes to choose from, maybe that will be the theme of the volume 2?

The mossy underside of the planter is deep brown, remember to put a shadow under it and on the wall in a purplish cast. Most flowers have a yellow center.

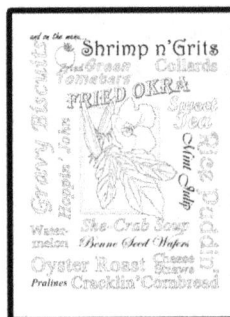

on the Menu

Southern favorites, just to name a few, please add your own.

Okra blossom is creamy white with a yellow center and a fading out deep red ring surrounding the center. Leaves in greens with a touch of burgundy red at sides and beginning of the leaf.

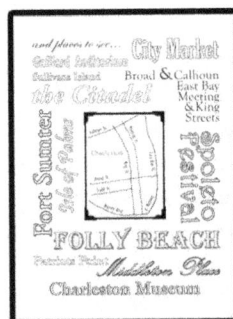

Places to See

This page could be colored, put on a mat, then add a favorite photo and frame for a great memory.

Choose a color family (ie. Yellow) make the words variations of it for color unity.

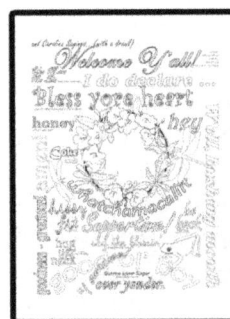

Sayings

Say with a drawl and blend right in, if y'all are not from around heah.

Add your own favorite saying or another butterfly in the center. Have fun!

A Carolina native, Judy Thompson-Phillips is a life long artist, starting very young with crayons and coloring books and now, *full circle back to coloring books!* The pages scenes are places that I have been to. Maybe you will discover where they are when next you tour beautiful Charleston.

A fine artist, Judy has original paintings, limited edition Giclee prints, notecards and mugs, most all with a Charleston influence.

"I truly hope you enjoy the pages in this book as much as I did making it for you"
Judy

Bonus Page
Sketch / sample colors